ENDANGERED ANIMALS AROUND THE WORLD

ENDANGERED REPTILES AROUND THE WORLD

BY GOLRIZ GOLKAR

PEBBLE
a capstone imprint

Published by Pebble, an imprint of Capstone
1710 Roe Crest Drive, North Mankato, Minnesota 56003
capstonepub.com

Copyright © 2025 by Capstone. All rights reserved. No part of this publication may be reproduced in whole or in part, or stored in a retrieval system, or transmitted in any form or by any means, electronic, mechanical, photocopying, recording, or otherwise, without written permission of the publisher.

Library of Congress Cataloging-in-Publication Data is available on the Library of Congress website.

ISBN: 9780756578343 (hardcover)
ISBN: 9780756578619 (paperback)
ISBN: 9780756578626 (ebook PDF)

Summary: From quick, strong crocodiles to lizards that just *look* like crocodiles, these endangered reptiles are having a tough time. Learn about some incredible reptiles that need our help to survive.

Editorial Credits
Editor: Ericka Smith; Designer: Sarah Bennett; Media Researcher: Svetlana Zhurkin; Production Specialist: Katy LaVigne

Image Credits
Alamy: Joe Blossom, 17, Wolfi Poelzer, 11; Getty Images: Ariel Skelley, 29; Shutterstock: Alexandros Michailidis, 6, Andrea Margutti, 19, Andrey Gudkov, 9, Andrzej Grzegorczyk, 15, Artush, 16, asantosg, 7, bayazed, 10, Danny Ye, cover, 21, David Jeffrey Ringer, 12, David Keep, 8, deannalindsey, 25, Dmitrii Kash, 4, Elvira Draat, 23, eric laudonien, 13, Kevin Wells Photography, 27, Kurit afshen, 5, Lawrence Cruciana, 26, Matteo photos, 18, Tanes Ngamsom, 22, Viacheslav Lopatin, 1

Any additional websites and resources referenced in this book are not maintained, authorized, or sponsored by Capstone. All product and company names are trademarks™ or registered® trademarks of their respective holders.

Printed and bound in China. 5827

TABLE OF CONTENTS

All About Endangered Reptiles 4

Cuban Crocodile 8

Grand Cayman Blue Iguana 12

Radiated Tortoise 14

Meadow Viper 18

Chinese Crocodile Lizard 20

Making Progress 24

How You Can Help 28

    Glossary 30

    Read More 31

    Internet Sites 31

    Index 32

    About the Author 32

Words in **bold** are in the glossary.

All About Endangered Reptiles

What Are Reptiles?

A snake slithers through the grass. It soaks up the warm sun. Snakes are reptiles.

Reptiles are **cold-blooded** animals. They get their body heat from their environment. They are **vertebrates** that usually lay eggs. Their dry skin has bony plates or scales. Most reptiles have short legs and long tails.

There are more than 8,700 reptile **species**. They include lizards, snakes, turtles, crocodiles, alligators, and chameleons. Reptiles are found on all continents except Antarctica.

What Is an Endangered Reptile?

About one in five reptile species is **endangered**. Some species are close to becoming **extinct**. They may die out.

Reptiles face many threats. People hunt them. Fishermen catch them by mistake. Farming, mining, and construction destroy their **habitats**. **Climate change** and wildfires are threats too.

Wildfires destroy animals and their habitats.

Where Do Endangered Reptiles Live?

There are endangered reptiles all over the world. Many are in danger because their habitats are being destroyed.

Here's where you can find the reptiles you'll learn about in this book!

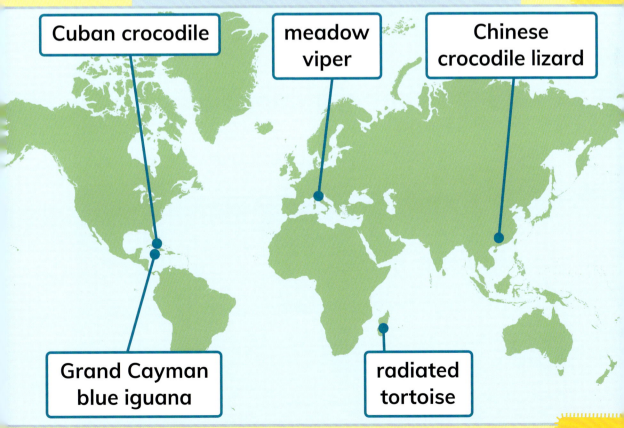

Cuban crocodile

meadow viper

Chinese crocodile lizard

Grand Cayman blue iguana

radiated tortoise

Cuban Crocodile

A Cuban crocodile soaks in a river. It looks for its next meal. *Snap!* Its giant jaws grab a fish.

Cuban crocodiles live in freshwater rivers and marshes. They are small but strong. They use their powerful tails to leap out of water. Then they grab animals to eat. Sometimes they attack people.

Cuban crocodiles face quite a few problems. People hunt them and use their skin to make products. Cuban crocodiles also have a small **range**. They only live in Cuba. This keeps their population low.

Cuban crocodiles on a breeding farm

American crocodiles have also entered their habitat. These two crocodiles sometimes **breed**. This creates a **hybrid** crocodile species. The number of pure Cuban crocodiles has gone down.

To help Cuban crocodiles, hunting and breeding must be controlled.

Grand Cayman Blue Iguana

Grand Cayman blue iguanas are big! They can weigh more than 20 pounds (9.1 kilograms). They are **native** to the island of Grand Cayman. They live mostly in dry, rocky forests.

These iguanas are endangered. Cats and dogs hunt them. Norway rats eat young iguanas. And people cut down the forests where they live. The iguanas have less of the plants and fruits they need to survive.

But some people are helping. Part of the iguana's habitat is protected. People are also breeding them and releasing the adults into the wild.

Radiated Tortoise

A radiated tortoise crawls in a forest. It munches a cactus plant. *Yum!*

These island tortoises are native to Madagascar. They are also found on the islands of Réunion and Mauritius.

Radiated tortoises are endangered. Many are **poached**. They are sold or hunted illegally. Some people eat them. Many think the tortoises are beautiful. They give people the tortoises as gifts.

Farming and mining have ruined their habitat. The tortoises have no place to live or graze for food. They can starve.

Native people help protect them. They stop members of their group from hurting the tortoises. Some take the tortoises home to help them. They protect them from dangers in the wild.

Miners in Madagascar

A zookeeper who helps breed radiated tortoises in Madagascar

Zoos are working with Native people too. They protect the tortoise's habitat. They also release poached animals into protected areas.

Meadow Viper

Meadow vipers live in grassy, rocky areas in Europe. They are **venomous**, but they're not a big threat to humans.

Sheep grazing where meadow vipers live

But these snakes face many threats. Wildfires burn their land. Farming and construction destroy their homes. Their environment is also polluted. Overgrazing and plant removal take away needed shrubs.

Meadow vipers are also caught and kept as pets. Some are killed to protect humans.

Chinese Crocodile Lizard

A Chinese crocodile lizard swims in a mountain stream. It darts around plants and rocky edges. Its tail is strong and scaly. It looks like a crocodile's tail.

Chinese crocodile lizards are in danger of dying out. They are the last surviving species of their lizard family. The family has existed for more than 100 million years.

Habitat loss is the main problem. The trees they need for shelter and protection are cut down. Coal mining harms their habitat. And dam construction makes it hard for the lizards to swim.

A coal-mining town in China

People are a threat in other ways too. Electrofishing uses shocks to catch fish. Lizards can be shocked by accident. People also illegally sell these lizards as pets. And some are hunted to make medicine.

But these lizards have some help. Part of their habitat is protected. Breeding programs are helping too.

Making Progress

American Alligator

In the 1960s, American alligators became endangered. People hunted them for their meat and skin.

But some people helped these alligators. They protected the wetlands where the alligators live. They bred and raised alligators. Then, they released them into the wild. They also banned hunting to protect the American alligator.

In 1987, the American alligator was removed from the endangered animals list. About five million of them now live in the southeastern United States.

Green Sea Turtle

In 1990, fewer than 50 green sea turtles had nests along Florida's eastern coast. People hunted them. Warming water temperatures made it harder for them to survive. Some were caught in fishing nets. And construction polluted their habitat.

People have helped prevent others from hunting the turtles. They helped fisheries stop trapping turtles by accident. And they found places where green sea turtles breed and eat. These places are better protected now.

By 2015, more than 12,000 nests were found in Florida. The turtles were coming back!

How You Can Help

Endangered reptiles need help to survive. Here's what you can do:

» Do not pollute water or soil with chemicals or trash.

» Do not buy products made from animals or tested on them.

» Do not choose wild animals as pets.

» Make sure your house pets do not disturb wildlife.

» Fight climate change: Use less electricity. Reduce, reuse, and recycle materials.

GLOSSARY

breed (BREED)—to mate and produce young

climate change (KLY-muht CHAYNJ)—a significant change in Earth's climate over a period of time

cold-blooded (KOHLD-BLUHD-id)—having a body that needs to get heat from its surroundings

endangered (en-DAYN-juhrd)—in danger of dying out

extinct (ek-STINGK)—no longer living

habitat (HAB-uh-tat)—the home of a plant or animal

hybrid (HY-brid)—bred from two different species

native (NAY-tuhv)—growing or living naturally in a place; from a group who originally lived in a place

poach (POHCH)—to hunt or fish illegally

range (RAYNJ)—where an animal mostly lives

species (SPEE-sheez)—a group of animals with similar features

venomous (VEN-uhm-us)—having or producing a poison called venom

vertebrate (VUR-tuh-brayt)—an animal with a backbone

READ MORE

Jaycox, Jaclyn. *Unusual Life Cycles of Reptiles.* North Mankato, MN: Capstone, 2022.

Nelson, Thomas. *Discovering Reptiles: The Ultimate Handbook to the Reptiles of the World!* Kennebunkport, ME: Applesauce Press, 2021.

Somaweera, Ruchira. *The Ultimate Book of Reptiles.* Washington, DC: National Geographic Kids, 2023.

INTERNET SITES

Britannica Kids: Reptile
kids.britannica.com/kids/article/reptile/353708

National Geographic Kids: Let's Make a Change: Habitat Destruction!
natgeokids.com/uk/kids-club/cool-kids/general-kids-club/lets-make-a-change-habitat-destruction

National Geographic Kids: Reptiles
kids.nationalgeographic.com/animals/reptiles

INDEX

American alligators, 24–25

Antarctica, 5

China, 22

Chinese crocodile lizards, 7, 20–23

climate change, 6, 26, 28

Cuba, 10

Cuban crocodiles, 7, 8–11

Europe, 18

Florida, 26, 27

Grand Cayman, 12

Grand Cayman blue iguanas, 7, 12–13

green sea turtles, 26–27

Madagascar, 14, 16, 17

Mauritius, 14

meadow vipers, 7, 18–19

radiated tortoises, 7, 14–17

Réunion, 14

United States, 24

ABOUT THE AUTHOR

Golriz Golkar is the author of more than 70 books for children. A former elementary school teacher, she holds degrees in American literature and literacy education. Golriz enjoys reading, cooking, singing with her daughter, and looking for ladybugs on nature walks.